Thomas Paine

Common Sense

◆ ABRIDGED & ANNOTATED ◆

With definitions and historical context
for students and modern readers

Edited by Brennen Ricks

For Clark (1975 - 2021), who taught me by his
example, conversation, and friendship.

To Christine, whose talents and support
made this possible.

To Dad, whose energy and love of history and truth
is contagious.

The first edition of *Common Sense* was published by Robert Bell on January 10, 1776
Philadelphia, Pennsylvania, USA

This book quotes from the February 14, 1776 edition of *Common Sense*
Published by W&T Bradford
Philadelphia, Pennsylvania, USA

Published in 2021 by Curly Design Co.
San Antonio, Texas, USA

ISBN 978-1-7343412-5-6

Cover design by Christine Ricks

Table of Contents

PREFACE

WHY WAS THIS LITTLE BOOK SO IMPORTANT?

Take yourself back to the summer in 1775. You're in Boston. Things are tense.

The Continental Army just fought to the last bullet, then in hand-to-hand combat, at Breeds Hill and Bunker Hill. The patriots inflicted almost three times as many casualties to the British than they received before falling back.

As a patriot, you're realizing we have a shot at independence, and the neighboring colonies are finding their courage.

But now it's winter. Your city is occupied by the British army and under siege by the Continental Army – there's nowhere to go.

You and everyone who came to the colonies for religious freedom or economic opportunity are faced with the same hard facts:

- Europe won't help us – we're a British colony, not a country they can make alliances with.
- The Native Americans won't help us – why should they? We fought against them and their French allies in a war just 12 years earlier.
- The King won't listen to us – and we have no representation, let alone allies, in Parliament.
- They tax us heavily, stripped our right to form our own laws, and force us to house British troops in our homes.
- Worst of all, we're bitterly divided amongst ourselves on what to do.

We are not a united nation.

Loyalists want to make amends and return to the status quo. Patriots want independence and to start something new. But the most problematic group is the remaining majority... They are uncommitted and indecisive on what stance to take.

But then on the 10th of January, 1776, a pamphlet is published anonymously in Philadelphia.

It reads like a sermon to Christians, and an economic and government plan to the colonists, and a rallying call for independence and revolution for the entire continent. It blasts the concept of monarchy and Kings. It exposes the false hopes of reconciliation with England. And it lays out the strength behind and reasons for a revolution for independence. It's a moral decision just as much as an economic or political one. It's "Common Sense."

And it spreads like wildfire.

George Washington requires his soldiers to read the pamphlet. It gets read out loud in taverns across the colonies. It sells over 100,000 copies in a few months. That's 1 copy for every 20 colonists - an incredible distribution. In just one year, it reaches over half a million copies sold worldwide. After nearly 250 years, it will remain the best-selling book ever printed in America, as a percentage of the population.

But as you read it, the last line says what you already know deep down to be true:

> "UNTIL AN INDEPENDENCE IS DECLARED, the Continent will feel itself like a man who continues putting off some unpleasant business...yet knows it must be done."

HOW WAS THIS ABRIDGED?

As an example, here's a paragraph from Common Sense before-and-after being abridged.

> **Original (130 words)**: "Government, like dress, is the badge of lost innocence; the palaces of kings are built on the ruins of the bowers of paradise. For were the impulses of conscience clear, uniform, and irresistibly obeyed, man would need no other lawgiver; but that not being the case, he finds it necessary to surrender up a part of his property to furnish means for the protection of the rest; and this he is induced to do by the same prudence which in every other case advises him out of two evils to choose the least. Wherefore, security being the true design and end of government, it unanswerably follows that whatever form thereof appears most likely to ensure it to us, with the least expence and greatest benefit, is preferable to all others."

> **Abridged with footnotes (106 words)**: "Government, like [wearing clothes], is the badge of lost innocence.[1] ...[Man] finds it necessary to surrender up a part of his property [to government] to furnish the means for protection of the rest. Wherefore, security being the true design and end of government, ...whatever form [of government] appears most likely to ensure it to us with the least expense and greatest benefit, is preferable to all others."

We didn't change Thomas Paine's message, arguments, or voice.

To make reading faster and easier to follow, we clarified uncommon words and modernized formatting a few ways:

- Modernized the spelling of words like Connexion, Expence,

---

1 "Lost Innocence" refers to how innocent little children don't feel embarrassed for not wearing clothes until they get older, but also refers to the biblical account of how Adam and Eve didn't feel ashamed for being naked until they were no longer innocent and "fell" from the Garden of Eden.

Reflexion, Favour, Parellels, and others.

- Replaced some Biblical or Shakespearian words like Hath or Shew with modern equivalents like Has or Shown.
- Split up 'run-on' sentences into separate, distinct sentences.
- Substituted or added words to make long sentences easily split up, and to replace difficult-to-understand phrases. Added words are in [thin brackets].
- Added footnotes or word-substitutions to define uncommon words such as Capricious, Magnanimity, Specious, etc. Substituted words are in [thin brackets].
- Formatted lists with bullet points, and added sub-headings to make long sections or lists easier to follow.

We did condense his paragraphs down to almost half the length by doing 3 things:

- Omitting repeated points
- Shortening lengthy examples or tangential thoughts.
- Condensed repetitious paragraphs to the main idea. Places where words were removed are shown by ellipsis "…"

How much easier did that make "Common Sense" to read?

Just condensing and reformatting sentences changes it from an advanced "college graduate and above" reading level to an "intelligent high school" reading level. Compare the before-and-after difficulty score across four different readability methods.

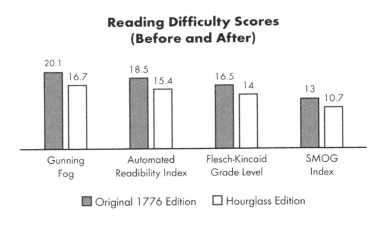

Reading Difficulty Scores (Before and After)

■ Original 1776 Edition   □ Hourglass Edition

How is this annotated?

Explanations and historical context are added as footnotes on each page to help simplify and add meaning to the difficult phrases or 18th century references.

Simple diagrams or tables were added for clarity, and some simplified tables replace more complex tables from the original work.

How much faster is this to read?

This takes less than half the time to read as the original, but doesn't take out any of Thomas Paine's main points. At times Thomas Paine used very long sentences, restated ideas multiple ways, and occasionally used phrases that carry very little

meaning today—250 years after they were written. Some of
those parts were able to be condensed.

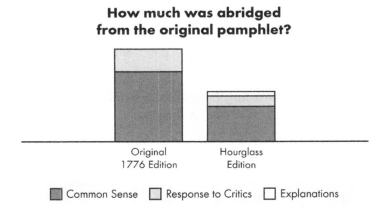

How much was abridged
from the original pamphlet?

Original
1776 Edition

Hourglass
Edition

■ Common Sense ☐ Response to Critics ☐ Explanations

This Hourglass Edition should let the average high-school level
reader shave this 2 to 4 hour long read down to about an hour,
not including however long you want to spend in the "historical
context" footnotes to better understand the people and events
Thomas Paine mentions.

What about the Declaration of Independence?

To many Americans, the Declaration of Independence is a
historical masterpiece somewhere between scripture and
poetry. This version adds definitions, explanations of phrases,
and improves the formatting without removing anything
meaningful. Making significant changes to the Declaration of
Independence wouldn't make it better, it would make it feel...
wrong.

We truly hope you put yourself in the place of the "undecided
majority" as you listen to Thomas Paine lay out his case for an
independent and democratic nation.

COMMON SENSE

Addressed to the Inhabitants of America on the following interesting subjects:

- The Origin and Design of Government...[and] the English Constitution
- Monarchy and Hereditary Succession
- The Present State of American Affairs
- The Present Ability of America

INTRODUCTION

The cause of America is, in a great measure, the cause of all mankind.

The laying of a country desolate with fire and sword, [and] declaring war against the natural rights of all mankind, ...is the concern of every man...given the power of feeling.

Who the author of this production is, is wholly unnecessary... as the object for attention is the doctrine itself, not the man[1]. Yet it [is necessary] to say that he is unconnected with any party and under no sort of influence...but the influence of reason and principle.

Philadelphia, February 14, 1776

---

1 Thomas Paine first published "Common Sense" anonymously (most likely out of caution from becoming a target of British loyalists) and the booklet's author remained anonymous for nearly three months. He didn't claim copyright at first publishing, so despite his efforts he didn't ever receive any money on its broad re-publication in other newspapers.

THE ORIGIN AND DESIGN OF GOVERNMENT, [AND] THE ENGLISH CONSTITUTION

Part 1:

Some writers have [confused] "society" with "government." ...They are not only different but have different origins.

Society is produced by our wants, and government by our wickedness.

The former promotes our happiness positively by uniting our affections, and [government promotes our happiness] negatively, by restraining our vices.

The one encourages [interaction], the other creates distinctions.

The first a patron *(meaning "a supporter")*, the last a punisher.

Society...is a blessing. But government, even in its best state, is but a necessary evil – in its worst state, an intolerable one.

Government, like [wearing clothes], is the badge of lost innocence.[2] [Mankind] finds it necessary to surrender up a part of his property [to government] to furnish the means for protection of the rest. Wherefore, security being the true design and [purpose] of government, ...whatever form [of government] appears most likely to ensure it to us with the least expense and greatest benefit, is preferable to all others.

In order to gain a clear and just idea of the design and end of government, let us suppose a small number of people settled in some sequestered part of the earth, unconnected with the rest. ...In this state of natural liberty, [forming] society will be their

---

2 "Lost Innocence" refers to how innocent little children don't feel embarrassed for not wearing clothes until they get older, but also refers to the biblical account of how Adam and Eve didn't feel ashamed for being naked until they were no longer innocent and "fell" from the Garden of Eden.

first thought ...[the] mind so unfitted for perpetual solitude. [They will] seek assistance and relief of another, who in his turn requires the same.

But as nothing...is [immune] to vice, it will unavoidably happen, ...they will begin to relax in their duty and attachment to each other. This...will point out the necessity of establishing some form of government to supply the defect of moral virtue.

But as the colony increases, the public concerns will increase... and the distance...will render it too inconvenient for all of them to meet on every occasion as at first when their numbers were small. This will point out the convenience of [the colony] consenting to leave the legislative part to be managed by a select number chosen from the whole body. [The select number] are supposed to have the same concerns at stake [as] those who appointed them, and will act...as the whole body would act [if] were they present.

Here then is the origin and rise *(or "cause")* of government: ... The inability of moral virtue to govern the world.

Here too is the design and end *(or "purpose")* of government: Freedom and security.

Part 2:

I draw my idea of the form of government from a principle in nature...that the more simple any thing is, the less [likely] it is to be [broken]; and the easier repaired when [broken]; With this maxim *(or "brief truth")* in view, I offer a few remarks on the "so much boasted" constitution of England.

It was noble for the dark times in which it was erected. ...But it is imperfect...and incapable of producing what it seems to promise.

The constitution of England is so exceedingly complex, that the nation may suffer for years...without being able to discover in which part the fault lies, ...and every "political physician" will advise a different medicine.

I know it is difficult to get over local or long-standing prejudices, yet if we...examine the component parts of the English constitution, we shall find them to be the remains of two ancient tyrannies, [mixed] with some new republic material.

(Summary of British branches of government)

The Monarch	Parliament	
King (from the Royal Family)	**House of Lords** (Noble families, plus a few Anglican Church bishops)	**House of Commons** (Delegates from counties in Great Britain)
Final Approval (or "Royal Assent") of bills into law	Reject or approve bills	Propose and pass bills

First - The remains of monarchical tyranny in the person of the King. [The Monarch]

Second - The remains of aristocratical tyranny in the persons of the Peers. [The House of Lords]

Third - The new republic material, in the persons of the Commons, on whose virtue depends the freedom of England. [The House of Commons]

The first two, by being hereditary *(or "passed from parent to child")*, are independent of the people. In a constitutional sense, they contribute nothing towards the freedom of the state.

To say that the constitution of England is a union of three powers reciprocally checking each other, is [not true]. Either the words have no meaning, or they are flat contradictions.

The prejudice of Englishmen, in favor of their own government by king, lords, and commons, arises as much or more from national pride than reason. ...But the will of the king is as much the law of the land in Britain as [the will of a king] in France, with this difference: [In England] instead of proceeding directly from [the king's] mouth, [the law] is handed to the people under the more formidable shape of an act of parliament. For the fate of Charles the First[3] has only made kings more subtle—not more just.

An inquiry into the constitutional errors in the English form of government is, at this time, highly necessary... As a man... attached to a prostitute is unfit to [be critical] of [his] wife, so any [previously held opinion] in favor of a rotten constitution of government will disable us from discerning a good one.

OF MONARCHY AND HEREDITARY SUCCESSION

Part 1:

Mankind [was] originally equal in the order of creation.

Equality could only be destroyed by some subsequent circumstance. The distinctions of rich and poor, may, in a great measure, account for [it]. ...Oppression is often the consequence [of riches], but seldom...the [way to] riches.

But there is another and greater distinction for which no... natural or religious reason can be assigned, and that is the distinction of men into kings and subjects.

...How a race of men came into the world so exalted above the rest...is worth inquiring into, and whether they are the means of happiness or of misery to mankind.

In the early ages of the world, according...to scripture, there were no kings; the consequence of which was there were no wars. It is the pride of kings which throw mankind into confusion.

---

3 "Charles the First" was a British king who, just over 100 years earlier, was perceived as a tyrant and eventually tried, convicted, and executed by the people for treason. The author suggests France's king doesn't hide being a tyrant, but the British king tries to hide his tyrannical rule through one layer of parliament like laundered money.

Holland, without a king, has enjoyed more peace for this last century than any of the monarchial governments in Europe.

Government by kings was first introduced into the world by the Heathens, from whom the children of Israel copied the custom. It was the most prosperous invention the Devil ever set on foot for the promotion of idolatry... *(meaning "the worship of things or people as deity")*

The exalting [of] one man so greatly above the rest cannot be justified on the equal rights of nature...neither can it be defended on the authority of scripture. For the will of the Almighty, as declared by Gideon[4] and the prophet Samuel,[5] expressly disapproves of government by kings.

Part 2:

All anti-monarchical parts of scripture have been smoothly glossed over in monarchical governments, but they...merit the attention of countries which have their governments yet to [be] formed.

[When Gideon and] the children of Israel [were] oppressed by the Midianites, Gideon marched against them with a small army [of 300]...The Jews elate with [Gideon's] success, and attributing it to the generalship of Gideon, proposed making him a king, saying: "Rule thou over us, thou and thy son and thy son's son."

Here was temptation in its fullest extent: [to be offered] not a kingdom only, but an hereditary one,

But Gideon...replied:

---

4 Gideon was a judge, military leader, and prophet of the biblical people of Israel around 1,200 years before Christ. The Bible records him dismissing his army of tens of thousands down to just 300 faithful and valiant men, who then defeat the Midianite army through divinely-inspired strategy.

5 Samuel is introduced in the Bible when called to be a prophet at 11 years old. Later, as a reputable leader and prophet, he led the oppressed Israelites to victory against the Philistines around 1,050 years before Christ.

"I will not rule over you, neither shall my son rule over you. The Lord shall rule over you." *(Old Testament, Judges 8:22-23)*

Gideon [didn't] decline the honor, but [denied] their right to give it; neither [did] he compliment them with...his thanks, but in the positive style of a prophet, charged them with disaffection to their proper Sovereign, the King of heaven.

About one hundred and thirty years after this, they fell again into the same error. They came in an abrupt and clamorous manner to Samuel, saying:

"Behold thou art old, and thy sons walk not in thy ways, now make us a king to judge us like all other nations. ... Samuel prayed unto the Lord, and the Lord said unto Samuel:

"Hearken unto the voice of the people in all that they say unto thee, for they have not rejected thee, but they have rejected me, THAT I SHOULD NOT REIGN OVER THEM. Wherewith they have forsaken me and served other Gods; so do they also unto thee. *(Old Testament, 1st Samuel 8:5-8)*

"And Samuel told all the words of the Lord unto the people, that asked of him a king.

"And [Samuel] said "This shall be the manner of the king that shall reign over you; he will take your sons and appoint them for himself...[to] run before his chariots. And [the king] will make his instruments of war, and instruments of his chariots; and he will take your daughters...to be cooks...and he will take your fields...and give them to his servants; and he will take the tenth of your feed, and of your vineyards, and give them to his officers...

And ye shall be his servants, and ye shall cry out in that day because of your king which ye shall have chosen, and the Lord will not hear you."

"Nevertheless the People refused...and they said: Nay, but

we will have a king over us, that we may be like all the nations."*(1st Samuel 8:11-19. Samuel will later identify Saul as the person to be the Israelite's king)*

"So Samuel called unto the Lord, and the Lord sent thunder and rain that day, and all the people greatly feared the Lord and Samuel. And all the people said unto Samuel, "Pray for thy servants unto the Lord thy God that we die not, for we have added unto our sins this evil, to ask a king." *(1st Samuel 12:19)*

To the evil of monarchy, we have added that of hereditary succession; ...For all men being originally equals, no one [has the] right to set up his own family [for] perpetual preference... for ever,

Part 3:

No man...without manifest injustice to their children, [could] say "Your children and your children's children shall reign over ours for ever." Most wise men, in their private sentiments, have ever treated hereditary right with contempt; yet it is one of those evils, ...once established, is not easily removed. Many submit from fear, ...and the more powerful part shares with the king the plunder of the rest.

[Some suppose]...kings in the world to have had an honorable origin; [But] it is more than probable, that [if we] could...trace them to their first rise, ...we [would] find the first of them nothing better than the principal ruffian of some restless gang, whose savage manners...[and] subtility obtained him the title of chief among plunderers.

Part 4:

England, since the conquest [of William the Conqueror], has known [a] few good monarchs, but groaned beneath a much larger number of bad ones; No [king]...can say that their claim under William the Conqueror is a very honorable one. A French bastard landing with an armed banditti, and establishing himself king of England against the consent of the natives, is in plain terms a very paltry rascally original.

...How [do] they suppose kings came at first? ...Either by lot,[6] by election, or by usurpation. If the first king was taken by lot, it establishes a precedent *(meaning "a pattern to follow")* for the next, which excludes hereditary succession. Saul was by lot,[7] yet the succession was not hereditary, neither...was [there] any intention it ever should.

If the first king of any country was by election, that likewise establishes a precedent for the next. ...Electors [choosing] not only of a king, but of a family of kings forever, has no parallel in or out of scripture.

As to usurpation - no man will be so hardy *(meaning "bold")* as to defend it. William the Conqueror was an usurper is a fact... [the] English monarchy will not bear looking into.

The evil of hereditary succession...concerns mankind.

[If] it ensured a race of good and wise [leaders] it would have the seal of divine authority. But...it has in it the nature of oppression. Men who look upon themselves born to reign, and others to obey, soon grow insolent. ...Their minds are early poisoned by importance. The world they act in differs so materially from the world at large, that they have but little opportunity of knowing [the world's] true interests. And when they succeed to the government, [they] are frequently the most ignorant and unfit...

Another evil which attends hereditary succession is that the throne is subject to be possessed by a minor at any age; The same national misfortune happens when a king, worn out with age

---

6 "by lot" means selecting using a fair, random process with dice or drawing straws, tossing sticks, etc.

7 The prophet Samuel told Saul privately that the Lord had chosen him to be king. Afterwards there was a public "casting of lots" where a randomized selection method using dice or sticks also chose Saul. This confirmed to Saul that if the people insisted on a king, it truly was the Lord's will for him to be the king.

and infirmity, enters the last stage of human weakness. In both these cases the public become prey to [those] who can tamper successfully with the follies of age or infancy.

The most plausible plea...in favor of hereditary succession is that it preserves a nation from civil wars. [That] is the most barefaced falsity... The whole history of England disowns the fact. Thirty kings and two minors have reigned in that distracted kingdom since the conquest [of William the Conqueror], in which time there have been...no less than eight civil wars and nineteen rebellions. Instead of making for peace, it...destroys [its] very foundation.

The nearer any government approaches to a republic, the less business there is for a king.

In England, a king has little more to do than to make war and give away places - which in plain terms, is to impoverish the nation ...A pretty business indeed for a man to be allowed eight hundred thousand sterling a year ...One honest man is of more worth to society - and in the sight of God - than all the crowned ruffians that ever lived.

THOUGHTS ON THE PRESENT STATE OF AMERICAN AFFAIRS

Part 1:

In the following pages I offer nothing more than simple facts, plain arguments, and common sense.

Volumes have been written on the subject of the struggle between England and America. Men of all ranks have embarked in the controversy...but all have been ineffectual, and the period of debate is closed.

Arms, as the last resource, decide the contest; the appeal [to arms] was the choice of the king, and the continent has accepted the challenge.

The sun never shined on a cause of greater worth. 'Tis not the affair of a city, a country, a province, or a kingdom, but of a continent. 'Tis not the concern of a day, or a year...posterity are virtually involved in the contest. Now is the seed time of continental union, faith, and honor. The [smallest] fracture now will be like a name engraved...on the tender young oak; the wound will enlarge with the tree...

A new era for politics is struck; a new method of thinking has arisen. All plans...prior to the nineteenth of April are superseded and useless now...[8]

Part 2:

[While] much has been said of the advantages of reconciliation, ...we should examine the contrary side of the argument and inquire into...the many material injuries which these colonies sustain and always will sustain by being connected with, and dependent on, Great Britain. [We should] examine that connection and dependance...to see what we have to [hope for], if separated, and what we are to expect, if dependent.

I have heard it asserted by some, that as America has flourished under her former connection with Great-Britain, that the same connection is necessary towards her future happiness... Nothing can be more [mistaken]...We may as well assert that because a child has thrived upon milk, that it is never to have meat. America would have flourished as much, and probably much more, [if] no European power had anything to do with her.

The commerce by which America has enriched herself are the necessities of life [such as food and materials], and will always

---

8 The previous night, Paul Revere and William Dawes were dispatched from Boston to warn of the coming British's plans to arrest patriot leaders John Hancock and Samuel Adams in Lexington, and to confiscate munitions in Concord. On the 19th of April of 1775, "Minute Men" militia met the British at Lexington. The first "shot heard round the world" at Lexington, then at Concord, were viewed as the opening battles of the Revolutionary War.

have a market while eating is the custom of Europe.

We have boasted the protection of Great-Britain, without considering that her motive was [self]-interest, not attachment; that she did not protect us from our enemies on our account, but from her enemies on her own account.

France and Spain never were, [and] perhaps never will be our enemies as Americans, but [would] as our being the subjects of Great-Britain.

Part 3:

"But Britain is the parent country," say some. Then the more shame upon her conduct. Even brutes do not devour their young, nor savages make war upon their families...

Europe, and not England, is the parent country of America. This new world has been the asylum for the persecuted lovers of civil and religious liberty from every part of Europe. They fled [to America], not from the tender embraces of the mother, but from the cruelty of the monster; and it is so far true of England, that the same tyranny which drove the first emigrants from home, pursues their descendants still.

We claim brotherhood with every European Christian, and triumph in the generosity of the sentiment. We surmount the force of local prejudice, as we enlarge our acquaintance with the world.

All Europeans meeting in America, or any other quarter of the globe, are countrymen; for England, Holland, Germany, or Sweden, when compared with the whole, stand in the same places on the larger scale. Divisions of street, town, and county [are] distinctions too limited for continental minds. Not one third of the inhabitants, even of this province, are of English descent. Wherefore I [disapprove] the phrase of "parent" or "mother country" applied to England only, as being false, selfish, narrow and ungenerous.

And to say that reconciliation is our duty, is truly [absurd]. The first king of England, of the present line *(William the Conqueror)* was a Frenchman, and half the Peers of England are descendants from the same country; therefore, by the same method of reasoning, England ought to be governed by France.

Besides, what have we to do with setting the world [against us]? Our plan is commerce! And that, well attended to, will secure us the peace and friendship of all Europe. It is the interest of all Europe to have America a free port. Her trade will always be a protection, and her barrenness of gold and silver secure her from invaders.

I challenge the warmest advocate for reconciliation to show a single advantage that this continent can reap by being connected with Great Britain. I repeat the challenge - not a single advantage is derived. Our corn will fetch its price in any market in Europe, and our imported goods must be paid for [wherever] we buy them.

But the injuries and disadvantages we sustain by that connection, are without number. Our duty to mankind at large, as well as to ourselves, instruct us to renounce the alliance...

Part 4:

Europe is too thick with kingdoms to be long at peace, and whenever a war breaks out between England and any foreign power, the trade of America goes to ruin because of her connection with Britain. The blood of the slain, the weeping voice of nature cries "Tis time to part!"

...The distance at which the Almighty has placed England and America is a strong and natural proof that the authority of the one, over the other, was never the design of Heaven.

The time...at which the continent was discovered adds weight to the argument, and the manner in which it was peopled increases the force of it.[9] The reformation was preceded by the

---

9 "The manner it was peopled" refers to the large amount of colonial immigrants who fled religious persecution from all across Europe.

discovery of America, as if the Almighty graciously meant to open a sanctuary to the persecuted in future years, when home should afford neither friendship nor safety.[10]

The authority of Great-Britain over this continent, is a form of government, which sooner or later must have an end.

As parents, we can have no joy knowing that this government is not sufficiently lasting to ensure anything which we may [leave] to posterity: And by a plain method of argument - as we are running the next generation into debt, we ought to do the work of [making a lasting government], otherwise we use them meanly and pitifully. In order to discover...our duty, we should take our children in our hand, and fix our [gaze] a few years farther into life.

Part 5:

I carefully avoid giving unnecessary offence, yet I am inclined to believe that all those who espouse the doctrine of reconciliation may be included within the following descriptions:

- [Self]-interested men, who are not to be trusted;
- Weak men, who cannot see;
- Prejudiced men, who will not see;
- And a certain set of moderate men, who think better of the European world than it deserves.[11]

This last class, by an ill-judged deliberation, will be the cause of more calamities to this continent than all the other three.

It is the good fortune of many to live distant from the scene

---

10 "The Reformation" refers to the era that started in the 1500s where Martin Luther, John Calvin, and others began to publicly question the authority of the Catholic Church and Pope on religion and politics. The Reformation focused the source of authority on scripture. But the new cultural freedoms came to Europe with a high cost of religious tensions and decades of non-stop wars.

11 "Moderate men" refers to the undecided and cautious group of people who were unsure about aligning with the British Loyalists or the Revolutionaries.

of sorrow... But let our imaginations transport us for a few moments to Boston.[12] The inhabitants of that unfortunate city, who but a few months ago were in ease and affluence, have no other alternative than to stay and starve or turn out to beg.

[They are] endangered by the fire of their friends if they continue within the city, and [risk being] plundered by the soldiery if they leave it. In their present condition they are prisoners without the hope of redemption. In a general attack for their relief, they would be exposed to the fury of both armies.

Men of passive tempers look somewhat lightly over the offences of Britain, and, still hoping for the best, ...call out, "Come, come, we shall be friends again..." But examine the passions and feelings of mankind...and then tell me, whether you can love, honor, and faithfully serve the power that has carried fire and sword into your land? If you cannot do all these, then are you only deceiving yourselves, and by your delay bringing ruin upon posterity.

But if you say you can still pass the violations over, then I ask: has your house been burnt? Has your property been destroyed before your face? Are your wife and children destitute of a bed to lie on, or bread to live on? Have you lost a parent or a child by their hands, and yourself the ruined and wretched survivor? If you have not, then are you not a judge of those who have.

But if you have, and still can shake hands with the murderers, then are you unworthy of the name of husband, father, friend, or lover. Whatever may be your rank or title in life, you have the heart of a coward.

I mean not to exhibit horror for the purpose of provoking revenge, but to awaken us from fatal and unmanly slumbers... It is not in the power of Britain or of Europe to conquer America,

---

12 In February of 1776, Boston was occupied by British troops and under siege by the Continental Army. The Battle of Bunker Hill had been fought nearby only a few months previously. It had been a violent, bloody fight. In its aftermath, the Continental Army surrounded Boston and pinned the British troops, as well as the Boston residents, in the city.

if [America] does not conquer herself by delay and timidity. The present winter is worth an age if rightly employed...

Reconciliation is now a fallacious dream. For, as Milton wisely expresses: "Never can true reconcilement grow where wounds of deadly hate have pierced so deep."[13]

Every quiet method for peace has been ineffectual. Our prayers have been rejected with disdain. [They] convince us that nothing flatters...Kings more than repeated petitioning. Since nothing but blows will do, for God's sake, let us come to a final separation, and not leave the next generation to be cutting throats...

Part 6:

As to government matters, it is not in the power of Britain to do this continent justice. The business of it will soon be too weighty and intricate to be managed...by a power so distant from us, and so very ignorant of us.

To be always running three or four thousand miles with...a petition, waiting four or five months for an answer (which when obtained requires five or six more to explain it in) will in a few years be looked upon as folly and childishness—

There was a time when it was proper, and there is a proper time for it to cease.

Small islands, not capable of protecting themselves, are the proper objects for kingdoms to take under their care; but there is something very absurd in supposing a continent to be perpetually governed by an island.

In no instance has nature made the satellite larger than its primary planet. England and America...[have] reversed the common order of nature. It is evident they belong to different systems: England to Europe, America to itself.

As Britain has not manifested [any] inclination towards a

---

13 John Milton was one of the most famous English poets in the late 1600s for writing the epic poem "Paradise Lost" about the fall of Adam and Eve.

compromise, we may be assured that no terms can be obtained worthy [of] the acceptance of the continent, or [in] any way equal to the expense of blood and treasure we have already put [out].

I am not induced by motives of pride, party, or resentment to espouse the doctrine of separation and independence; I am clearly persuaded that it is the true interest of this continent to be so. Everything short of [independence] is mere patchwork. It is leaving the sword to our children, and shrinking back...when a little farther would have rendered this continent the glory of the earth.

The object contended for, ought [to be in] proportion to the expense. Dearly, dearly, do we pay for the repeal of the acts.[14] If that is all we fight for, ...it is as great a folly to pay a Bunker-hill price for law.[15]

...It was not worth the while to have disputed a matter...unless we meant to be in earnest; otherwise, it is like wasting an estate on a [lawsuit to evict] a tenant, whose lease is just expiring.

No man was a warmer wisher for reconciliation than myself,

---

14 A number of laws or "acts" forced on the colonists grew from disagreeable to oppressive. The disagreeable acts included a group of four taxes in 1767 called the Townshend Acts. American resistance to taxes on British imports resulted in additional British troops stationed in Boston, as well as the colonists' formation of the "Daughters of Liberty," and boycotts of British goods. All of the Townshend Acts, except the tax on Tea, were repealed in 1770. But after the Boston Tea Party in December 1773, another shock came as England passed a set of five oppressive laws called the "Coercive Acts" in an attempt to isolate Boston and stop rebellious activities. The laws closed the Boston port, prohibited town meetings, made British officers immune from criminal prosecution, and forced locals to house British soldiers in their homes if needed.

15 The "price" paid at Bunker Hill was a violent, bloody battle. Primarily fought at Breeds Hill, The Continental Army ran out of ammunition, but stood their ground in hand-to-hand combat until forced to retreat. The colonists suffered heavy casualties but inflicted over twice the amount of casualties to the British. While technically a defeat, it was a morale-boosting display of strength for the Continental Army, and wake-up call to the British leadership.

before the fatal nineteenth of April. But the moment the event of that day was made known, I rejected the...Pharaoh of England forever. [I] disdain the wretch [because he] with the pretended title of "father of his people" can unfeelingly hear of their slaughter, and composedly sleep with their blood upon his soul.

Part 7:

But admitting that "matters [are] now made up," what would be the [result]?

I answer, "The ruin of the continent...for several reasons."

First: Is there any inhabitant in America so ignorant not to know, according to...the present constitution, this continent can make no laws but what the king gives [consent] to? And...he will suffer no law to be made here, but such as suit his purpose.

Can there be any doubt, but the whole power of the crown will be exerted to keep this continent as low and humble as possible? ...We are already greater than the king wishes us to be, and will he not endeavor to make us less? To bring the matter to one point: Is the power who is jealous of our prosperity, a proper power to govern us?

The king's negative [influence] here is ten times more dangerous and fatal than it can be in England. For there he will scarcely refuse his consent to a bill [that puts] England into as strong a state of defense as possible, [but] in America he would never suffer such a bill to be passed.

America is only a secondary object in the system of British politics... [England's] own interest leads her to suppress the growth of ours in every case which does not promote her advantage.

In order to show that reconciliation now is a dangerous doctrine, I affirm, that it would be policy in the king to repeal the acts...in order that he may accomplish by craft and subtilty, in the long run, what he cannot do by force and violence in the short [run]. Reconciliation and ruin are [closely] related.

Second: The best terms, which we can expect to obtain, [will be] no more than a temporary...government by guardianship, which can last no longer than [until] the colonies come of age.

So the general...state of things, in the interim, will be unsettled and unpromising. Emigrants...will not choose to come to a country whose form of government hangs by a thread, ... tottering on the brink of commotion and disturbance. And numbers of the present inhabitants would...dispense...and quit the continent.

But the most powerful of all arguments, is, that nothing but independence - a continental form of government - can keep the peace of the continent and preserve it inviolate *(or "safe from injury")* from civil wars. I dread the event of a reconciliation with Britain...will be followed by a revolt somewhere, the consequences, of which, may be far more fatal than all the malice of Britain.

A government which cannot preserve the peace is no government at all. In that case, we pay our money for nothing; ...for there [is] ten times more to dread from a patched-up connection than from independence.

I make the sufferer's case my own. I protest, that were I driven from house and home, my property destroyed, and my circumstances ruined, that...I could never relish the doctrine of reconciliation, or consider myself bound thereby.

[An Initial Plan]

If there is any true cause of fear respecting independence, it is because no plan is yet laid down.

I offer the following hints...that they may be the means of giving rise to something better - material for wise and able men to improve.

(Diagram of Paine's proposed republic)

	(Local) **House of Assembly**	(National) **Continental Congress**	(National) **President**
VA	👤👤👤👤👤	👤👤👤	
PA	👤👤👤👤👤👤	👤👤👤	👤 Congress votes on who is president.
MD	👤👤👤👤👤👤	👤👤👤	
MA	👤👤👤👤👤	👤👤👤	The colonies take turns providing candidates from their current pool of representatives.
NY	👤👤👤👤👤	👤👤👤👤	
GA	👤👤👤👤👤	👤👤👤	
NC	👤👤👤👤👤	👤👤👤	
CT	👤👤👤	👤👤👤	
SC	👤👤👤	👤👤👤👤	
NJ	👤👤👤	👤👤👤	
NH	👤👤👤	👤👤👤	
DE	👤👤👤	👤👤👤	
RI	👤👤👤	👤👤👤	
	(House and Congress reps could be the same people)		

- Let the assemblies be annual, with a President only. The representation more equal. Their business wholly domestic, and subject to the authority of a Continental Congress.
- Let each colony be divided into...districts, each district to send a proper number of delegates to Congress... The whole number in Congress will be at least 390.
- Congress [will] choose a president by the following method: [One] colony be taken from the whole thirteen colonies by lot *(meaning "random selection"),* after which, let the whole Congress choose (by ballot) a president from out of the

delegates of that [one] province. In the next Congress, let a colony be taken by lot...omitting [the first]...so proceeding on till the whole thirteen shall have had their [turn providing the presidential candidates].

- For something to] pass into a law, ...three fifths of the Congress [will] be called a majority.

—He that will promote discord, under a government so equally formed as this, would have joined Lucifer in his revolt.[16]

[Call for a Constitutional Convention]

[For] this business [to] first arise...from some intermediate body...let a Continental Conference be held, in the following manner, and for the following purpose:

- Two members from each House of Assembly or Provincial Convention, and five representatives of the people at large, [shall] be chosen in the capital city or town of each province, for...the whole province. ...The members of Congress, Assemblies, or Conventions...will be able and useful counsellors. The whole, being impowered by the people, will have a truly legal authority.
- Let their business be to frame a Continental Charter, or Charter of the United Colonies (answering to what is called the Magna Carta of England):
  - Fixing the number and manner of choosing members of Congress, members of Assembly.
  - Drawing the line of business and jurisdiction between them (Always remembering, that our strength is continental, not provincial).
  - Securing freedom and property to all men, and above all things, the free exercise of religion, according to the dictates of conscience.
  - Other matters as necessary...for a charter to contain.
- Immediately after, ...the Conference [will] dissolve, and the

16 The "revolt" refers to chapter 12 in the New Testament Book of Revelation, where Lucifer (a.k.a. Satan, or the Devil) led a third of the angles in heaven in a revolt against God, and were cast out.

bodies which shall be chosen conforming to the charter, [will] be the legislators and governors of this continent for the time being - Whose peace and happiness, may God preserve. Amen.

Should any body of men be hereafter delegated for this... purpose, I offer them the following:

"The science...of the politician consists in fixing the true point of happiness and freedom. Those men would deserve the gratitude of ages, who should discover a mode of government that contained the greatest sum of individual happiness, with the least national expense." -Dragonetti on Virtue and Rewards.[17]

[Returning to Present State]

"But where," some say, "is the King of America?" I'll tell you, Friend - He reigns above, and does not make havoc of mankind like the Royal Brute of Britain. ...In America the law is king. In absolute governments the King is law; In free countries the law ought to be King.

A government of our own is our natural right: And when a man seriously reflects on the precariousness of human affairs, he will become convinced, that it is infinitely wiser and safer to form a constitution of our own, in a cool, deliberate manner, while we have it in our power.

Ye that oppose independence now, ye know not what ye do; You are opening a door to eternal tyranny, by keeping vacant the seat of government. To talk of friendship with those in whom our reason forbids us to have faith...is madness and folly.

Ye that tell us of harmony and reconciliation, can ye restore to us the time that is past? Can you give to prostitution its former

---

17 Giacinto Dragonetti was a judge in Italy who published a book in 1766 called "A Treatise on Virtues and Rewards." The book discusses a theory about how people ultimately do virtuous things out of self-interest, so you might as well create incentives for good behavior.

innocence? Neither can you reconcile Britain and America. The last cord now is broken. The Almighty has implanted in us these unextinguishable feelings for good and wise purposes. The robber, and the murderer, would often escape unpunished, [if] the injuries...[didn't] provoke us into justice.

O ye that love mankind, ye that dare oppose, not only the tyranny, but the tyrant, stand forth! Every spot of the old world is overrun with oppression. Freedom has been hunted round the globe. Asia, and Africa, have long expelled her—Europe regards her like a stranger, and England has given her warning to depart. O! Receive the fugitive, and prepare in time a [refuge] for mankind!

THE PRESENT ABILITY OF AMERICA

Part 1:

I have never met with a man, either in England or America, who has not confessed his opinion, that a separation between the countries, would take place one time or another.

It is not in numbers, but in unity, that our great strength lies; yet our present numbers are sufficient to repel the force of all the world. The Continent has, at this time, the largest body of armed and disciplined men of any power under Heaven; and is just arrived at that pitch of strength, ...and the whole, when united, can accomplish the matter, and...might be fatal in its effects. Our land force is already sufficient...[but] Britain would never suffer an American Man-of-War to be built, while the continent remained in her hands.[18]

Were the continent crowded with inhabitants, her sufferings under the present circumstances would be intolerable. Our present numbers are so happily proportioned to our wants, that no man need be idle. The [reduction] of trade [justifies having] an army, and the necessities of an army create a new trade.

Part 2:

Debts we have none; and whatever we [incur to build an army or navy] will serve as a glorious memento of our virtue.

Can we [do anything] but leave posterity with a settled form of government - an independent constitution of its own? The purchase at any price will be cheap.

But to expend millions for the sake of getting a few vile acts repealed, and routing the present ministry only, is unworthy the charge - leaving [posterity] a debt upon their backs, from which they derive no advantage.

Britain is oppressed with a debt of upwards of one hundred and forty millions sterling, for which she pays upwards of four million in interest.[19] And as a compensation for her debt, she has a large navy; America is without a debt, and without a navy; yet for the twentieth part of the English national debt, could have a

---

18 A "Man-of-War" was a large Royal Navy warship, often with 3 decks of up to 100 (or more) cannons each capable of shooting a solid 32-pound ball of iron. For perspective, both General Washington's army and the British army each had just a few dozen cannons or less in action during the key battles in 1776. When Washington crossed the Delaware on Christmas Day in 1776, his 18 cannons were 3 times the firepower of the opposition. A single naval Man-of-War had more firepower against any costal town or enemy ship than both armies' field artillery combined.

19 One pound sterling in 1776 would be about 160 pound sterling today, so 140 million sterling back then is almost 22.5 billion sterling or $30.5 billion US dollars today. This was big debt for the era because countries and economies were a lot smaller, so coming up with that money to pay back the debt would be burdensome – and the debt was incurring interest.

navy as large again.

The navy of England is not worth, at this time, more than three and an half million sterling. The first and second editions of this pamphlet were published without the following calculations, which are now given as a proof that the above estimation of the navy is just. (See Entic's naval history)[20]

The charge of building a ship of each rate, and furnishing her with masts, yards, sails and rigging, together with a proportion of eight months boatswain's and carpenter's sea-stores, as calculated by Mr. Burchett, Secretary to the navy.

(Abridgement of the calculations)

British Ships	Average Price (Per Ship)	Total Price
251 Man-of-War gunships	12,338 Sterling each	3,096,838 Sterling
85 small ships	2,000 Sterling each	170,000 Sterling
Cost of All Ships		3,266,838 Sterling
Guns and Supplies		233,162 Sterling
Total Value of British Navy		3,500,000 Sterling

Part 3:

No country on the globe is so happily situated, or so internally capable of raising a fleet as America. Tar, timber, iron, and cordage are her natural produce. We need |to| go abroad for nothing.

We ought to view...building a fleet as an article of commerce, it being the natural manufactory of this country. It is the best money we can lay out. A navy when finished is worth more

---

20 "Entic's Naval History" was an almanac that recorded the cost of different types of naval ships, depending on the type and number of guns they held.

than it cost. And is that nice point in national policy, in which commerce and protection are united.

Let us build! If we want them not, we can sell [them], and by that means replace our paper currency with ready gold and silver.[21]

Wherefore, we never can be more capable to begin on maritime matters than now, while our timber is standing, our fisheries blocked up, and our sailors and shipwrights out of employ. Men-of-War, of seventy and eighty guns, were built forty years ago in New-England. Why not the same now?

Ship-building is America's greatest pride, and in which, she will in time excel the whole world. The great empires of the East are mostly inland, and [are] consequently excluded from the possibility of rivalling her. ...No power in Europe, has either such an extent of coast, or such an internal supply of materials. Where nature has given the one [materials], she has withheld the other [access to the ocean]; to America only has she been liberal of both.

In point of safety, ought we to be without a fleet? We are not the little people now, which we were sixty years ago. At that time we might have trusted our property in the streets, or fields rather; and slept securely without locks or bolts to our doors or windows. The case now is altered, and our...defense ought to improve with our increase of property. ...Any daring fellow, in a brig of fourteen or sixteen guns, might have robbed the whole Continent, and carried off half a million of money. These are circumstances which demand our attention, and point out the necessity of naval protection.

Part 4:

Some, perhaps, will say: "After we have made it up with Britain,

---

21 Each colony had their own paper currency. Not all colonies accepted each other's printed money, and little of the paper money was backed by actual gold or silver. A country-wide American dollar and mints to produce standard gold, silver and copper coins didn't come around until 16 years later when President Washington signed the Coinage Act of 1792 into law.

she will protect us." Can we be so unwise |to believe| that she shall keep a navy in our harbors? Common sense will tell us that the power which |she| has endeavored to subdue us, is...the most improper to defend us. And if her ships are not...in our harbors, ...how is she to protect us? A navy three or four thousand miles off can be of little use, and on sudden emergencies, none at all.

The East and West Indies, Mediterranean, Africa, and other parts over which Britain extends her claim, make large demands upon her navy. ...We have contracted a false notion respecting the navy of England, |that| we should have the whole of it to encounter at once - and...supposed that we must have one as large; ...Nothing can be farther from truth than this.

For if America had only a twentieth part of the naval force of Britain, she would be, by far, |a| match for her because...our whole force would be employed on our own coast. We should... have two-to-one the advantage of those who had three or four thousand miles to sail over, before they could attack us, and the same distance to return in order to refit and recruit.

And although Britain, by her fleet, has |leverage| over our trade to Europe, we have as large a one over her trade to the West-Indies, which...is entirely at its mercy.

Part 5:

Method might be...to keep up a naval force in time of peace. If |payments| were to be given to merchants, to...employ in their service ships mounted with...guns, |then| fifty or sixty of those ships, with a few guardships on constant duty, would keep up a sufficient navy. And |it would do| that without burdening ourselves with the evil so loudly complained of in England, of suffering their fleet in time of peace to lie rotting in the docks. To unite...commerce and defense is sound policy; for when our strength and our riches play into each other's hand, we need fear no external enemy.

Wherefore, what is it that we want? Why is it that we hesitate?

We are sufficiently numerous, and were we more so, we might

be less united.

Part 6:

It is a matter worthy of observation, …[that] men become too much absorbed [by commerce] to attend to anything else. Commerce diminishes the spirit, both of patriotism and military defense. And history sufficiently informs us, that the bravest achievements were always accomplished in the [youth] of a nation. With the increase of commerce, England has lost its spirit. The city of London…submits to continued insults with the patience of a coward. The more men have to lose, the less willing are they to venture. The rich are (in general) slaves to fear… Youth is the seed time of good habits, as well in nations as in individuals.

The present time…is that peculiar time, which never happens to a nation but once - The time of forming itself into a government. Most nations have let slip the opportunity, and by that means have been compelled to receive laws from their conquerors.

Instead of making laws for themselves, first they had a king, and then a form of government; whereas, the articles of… government should be formed first, and men delegated to execute them afterward.

Part 7:

As to religion, I hold it to be the indispensable duty of all government, to protect all conscientious professors thereof.

For myself, I fully and conscientiously believe, that it is the will of the Almighty, that there should be diversity of religious opinions among us. It affords a larger field for our Christian kindness. Were we all of one way of thinking, our religious dispositions *(or "beliefs")* would want matter for probation.[22] On this liberal principle, I look on the various denominations among us, to be like children of the same family, differing only, in what is called, their Christian names.

Part 8:

To Conclude...many strong and striking reasons may be given that nothing can settle our affairs so expeditiously as an open and determined DECLARATION FOR INDEPENDENCE.

Some of which are:

First – It is the custom of nations, when any two are at war, for some other powers, not engaged in the quarrel, to step in as mediators, and bring about [talks] of a peace: but while America calls herself the Subject of Great-Britain, no power...can offer her mediation. Wherefore, in our present state we may quarrel on forever.

Second—It is unreasonable...that France or Spain will give us any kind of assistance, if we mean only to make use of that assistance for the purpose of [reconciliation], and strengthening the connection between Britain and America; because, [France or Spain] would be sufferers [of] the consequences.

Third—We must, in the eye of foreign nations, be considered as rebels. [Professing ourselves the subjects of Britain] is somewhat dangerous to [a foreign nations'] peace.

Fourth—WERE A MANEFESTO TO BE PUBLISHED, and dispatched to foreign courts, setting forth:

1. The miseries we have endured
2. The peaceable methods we have ineffectually used for redress

22 "Wanting matter for probation" refers to needing a motive to prove your faith to yourself and others. If everyone is a part of the same state-imposed religion (like the Church of England), then there isn't an opportunity to prove how kind you will be to others who are of a different faith.

3. Declaring...we had been driven to the necessity of breaking off all connections with her

4. Assuring all such courts of our peaceable disposition towards them, and of our desire of entering into trade with them...

Such a memorial would produce more good effects to this Continent than if a ship were freighted with petitions to Britain.

[As] British subjects, we can neither be received nor heard abroad: The custom of all courts is against us, and will be so, until by an independence, we take rank with other nations.

These proceedings may at first appear strange and difficult; but, like all other steps which we have already passed over, will in a little time become familiar and agreeable; and, UNTIL AN INDEPENDENCE IS DECLARED, the Continent will feel itself like a man who continues putting off some unpleasant business from day to day, yet knows it must be done.

APPENDIX

[THOMAS PAINE'S RESPONSE TO RELIGIOUS PACIFISTS]

Historical Context: British Loyalists published a short response to Common Sense just 10 days after the first edition made its debut. The critical response advocated for reconciliation, abstaining from war, and being subject to the King on moral grounds, and "abhorrence of all such writings" such as Common Sense that encouraged the "desire...to break the happy connection we have heretofore enjoyed with the kingdom of Great Britain." It was signed on behalf of the conference of Quakers by John Pemberton, a wealthy and prominent figure at the time.

Part 1:

TO THE REPRESENTITIVES OF THE RELIGIOUS SOCIETY OF THE PEOPLE CALLED QUAKERS,[1] or [to them] concerned in publishing the [recent] piece, entitled:

"The Ancient Testimony and Principles of the People called Quakers renewed, with Respect to the King and Government, and touching the Commotions now prevailing in these and other parts of America addressed to the People in General."

THE WRITER OF THIS is one of those few who never dishonors religion either by ridiculing, or [making petty objections] at any

---

1 Quakers are a Christian faith who beliefs include refusal to participate in war (also called "Pacifism" or "Conscientious Objection").

denomination whatsoever. To God, and not to man, are all men accountable on the score of religion.

Wherefore, this epistle *(or "letter")* is not...addressed to you as a religious [group], but as a political body...

As you have...put yourselves in the place of the whole body of the Quakers, ...the writer of this...is under the necessity of putting himself in the place of all those who approve the very writings and principles, against which your testimony is directed:

And he has chosen this singular situation, in order that you might discover in him that presumption of character which you cannot see in yourselves.

Part 2:

And it is evident...that politics (as a religious body of men) is not your proper walk; [Your testimony] is...a jumble of good and bad put unwisely together, and the conclusion drawn therefrom, both unnatural and unjust.

The two first pages, ...we give you credit for, and expect the same civility from you, because the love and desire of peace is not confined to Quakerism;[2] it is the natural [and] religious wish of all denominations of men.

...As men laboring to establish an Independent Constitution of our own, do we exceed all others in our hope, end, and aim. Our plan is peace for ever.

We are tired of contention with Britain, and can see no real end to it but in a final separation. ...For the sake of introducing an endless and uninterrupted peace, do we bear the evils and burdens of the present day.

We fight neither for revenge, nor conquest; neither from pride, nor passion.

We are not insulting the world with our fleets and armies, nor

---

2 The first 2 of the 3 ½ pages were about the peaceful nature of Jesus Christ.

ravaging the globe for plunder.

Beneath the shade of our own vines are we attacked. In our own houses, and on our own lands, is the violence committed against us. We view our enemies in the character of...housebreakers, and having no defense for ourselves in the civil law, are obliged to punish them by the military one...

Perhaps we feel for the ruined and insulted sufferers in all and every part of the continent, with a degree of tenderness which has not yet made its way into some of your [hearts].

But...mistake not the cause and ground of your Testimony. Call not coldness of soul "religion," or put the Bigot in the place of the Christian.

Part 3:

O ye partial ministers of your own acknowledged principles... If ye really preach from conscience, and mean not to make a political hobby-horse of your religion, convince the world thereof, by proclaiming your doctrine to our enemies, for they likewise bear arms. Give us proof of your sincerity by publishing it at St. James's,[3] to the commanders in chief at Boston, to the Admirals and Captains who, [like pirates], are ravaging our coasts.

Had ye the honest soul...ye would preach repentance to your king; Ye would tell the Royal Wretch his sins, and warn him of eternal ruin. Ye would not spend your partial invectives (*meaning "critical one-sided comments"*) against the injured and the insulted only, but, like faithful ministers, would cry aloud and spare none.

Say not that ye are persecuted [by us], ...for we testify unto all men, that we do not complain against you because ye are

---

3 St. James' Palace (also called St. James' Place) was a mansion owned by King George I and II. King George III would later buy Buckingham House for his queen because he didn't think St. James Place was sufficiently private or suitable enough.

Quakers, but because ye pretend to be and are not Quakers.

It seems by...your testimony...as if, all sin was reduced to...the act of bearing arms, and by [us] only.

Ye appear to us to have mistaken [political] party for conscience.

Part 4:

The quotation from Proverbs in the third page of your testimony, that, "when a man's ways please the Lord, he maketh even his enemies to be at peace with him" is very unwisely chosen... because, it amounts to a proof that the king's ways (whom ye are desirous of supporting) do not please the Lord. Otherwise, his reign would be in peace.

I now proceed to the latter part of your testimony:

> "It has ever been our judgment and principle...that the setting up and putting down kings and governments, is God's peculiar prerogative; ...And that it is not our business...but to pray for the king, and safety of our nation, and good of all men: That we may live a peaceable and quiet life...under the government which God is pleased to set over us."

If these are really your principles, why do ye not abide by them? Why do ye not leave...God's work to be managed by himself? These very principles instruct you to wait with patience and humility... What occasion is there for your political testimony...? The very publishing [of] it proves...ye do not believe what ye profess, or have not virtue enough to practice what ye believe.

Kings are not taken away by miracles, neither are changes in governments brought about by any other means than such as are common and human; and such as we are now using. Even the dispersion of the Jews, though foretold by our Savior, was effected by arms.

Part 5:

Wherefore, as ye refuse to be the means on one side, ye ought not to be meddlers on the other; but to wait the issue in silence.

Unless ye can produce divine authority to prove that the Almighty...disapproves of [this place] being independent of the corrupt and abandoned court of Britain, ...how can ye on the ground of your principles, justify the exciting and stirring up the people "firmly to unite in the abhorrence of all such writings, and measures, as evidence a desire and design to break off the happy connection we have hitherto enjoyed, with the kingdom of Great-Britain, and our just and necessary subordination to the king, and those who are lawfully placed in authority under him?"

What a slap of the face is here!

The [same] men, who in the very paragraph before have quietly and passively resigned disposal of kings and governments into the hands of God, are now recalling their principles, and putting in for a share of the business. ...The inconsistency is too glaring not to be seen. ...For ye are not to be considered as the whole body of the Quakers but only as a factional and fractional part thereof.

Part 6:

Here ends the examination of your testimony, which I call upon no man to abhor, as ye have done, but only to read and judge of fairly. ...Your testimony, in whatever light it is viewed, serves only to dishonor your judgement.

For many other reasons [it was best] let alone than published:

- Because it tends to the decrease...all religion whatever, and is of the utmost danger to society to make it a party in political disputes.
- Because it has a tendency to undo that continental harmony and friendship which yourselves...have lent a hand to establish;

And here without anger or resentment I bid you farewell. Sincerely wishing, that as men and Christians, ye may always fully and uninterruptedly enjoy every civil and religious right; and be, in your turn, the means of securing it to others;

But that the example which ye have unwisely set, of mingling religion with politics, may be disavowed...by every inhabitant of America.

[THOMAS PAINE'S RESPONSE TO KING GEORGE III'S SPEECH TO PARLIAMENT]

Historical Context: *The Continental Congress sent a petition for peace and expressing the desire to be loyal to the king in a letter called the "Olive Branch Petition" in 1775. King George III received it in September, then spoke to the British Parliament on October 26, 1775 where he mocked and criticized the petition as disingenuous. He told Parliament that order needed to be restored, suggested most loyalists in the colonies were just laying low until more support from Britain arrived, and showed his permission to dispatch more soldiers to the colonies.*

Part 1:

SINCE THE PUBLICATION OF THE FIRST EDITION of this pamphlet, or rather, on the same day on which it came out, the King's Speech made its appearance in this city. ...And the Speech, instead of terrifying, prepared a way for the manly principles of Independence.

...It is often better, to pass some things over in silent disdain. ...Perhaps, it is chiefly owing to this prudent delicacy that the King's Speech has not, before now, suffered a public execution.

The Speech (if it may be called one) is nothing better than a

THE DECLARATION OF INDEPENDENCE

In Congress, July 4, 1776

The Unanimous Declaration of the Thirteen United States of America:

WHEN IN THE COURSE OF HUMAN EVENTS, it becomes necessary for one people to dissolve the political bands which have connected them with another - and to assume among the powers of the earth, the separate and equal station to which the Laws of Nature and of Nature's God entitle them,

A decent respect to the opinions of mankind requires that they should declare the causes which impel them to the separation.

We hold these truths to be self-evident:

- That all men are created equal, that they are endowed by their Creator with certain unalienable rights, that among these are Life, Liberty, and the pursuit of Happiness.
- That to secure these rights, governments are instituted among Men, deriving their just powers from the consent of the governed.
- That whenever any form of government becomes destructive of these ends, it is the right of the people to alter or to abolish it, and to institute new government - laying its foundation on such principles and organizing its powers in such form, as to them shall seem most likely to effect their safety and happiness.

Prudence, indeed, will dictate that governments long established should not be changed for light and transient causes; and accordingly, all experience has shown that mankind is more disposed to suffer, (while evils are sufferable) than to right themselves by abolishing the forms to which they are accustomed. But when a long train of abuses and usurpations, pursuing invariably the same object [reveals] a design to reduce them under absolute Despotism, it is their right - it is their duty - to throw off such government, and to provide new guards for their future security.

Such has been the patient sufferance of these Colonies; and such is now the necessity which constrains them to alter their former systems of government. The history of the present King of Great Britain is a history of repeated injuries and usurpations,[1] all having in direct object the establishment of an absolute Tyranny over these States.

To prove this, let facts be submitted to a candid world.

[Section 1 - Intentional Neglect]

- He has refused his Assent to Laws,[2] [ones that are] the most wholesome and necessary for the public good.
- He has forbidden his governors to pass laws of immediate and pressing importance, unless suspended ...until his approval should be obtained; and when so suspended, he has utterly neglected to attend to them.
- He has refused to pass other laws for the accommodation of large districts of people, unless those people would relinquish the right of representation in the legislature - a right inestimable to them, and formidable[3] to tyrants only.

[Section 2 - Reducing Rights]

- He has called together legislative bodies at places unusual, uncomfortable, and distant from the depository of their public records, for the sole purpose of fatiguing them into

---

1 An illegitimate claim to power.

2 "Assent to Law" means approval or recognition of a law. The colonies had a parliament that would propose laws, but the proposals would only go into effect if the British king approved them. King George III continuously refused to recognize their proposals.

3 "Formidable" meaning something that inspires fear or respect by being powerful and impressive.

Maryland

- Samuel Chase
- William Paca
- Thomas Stone
- Charles Carroll of Carrollton

Virginia

- George Wythe
- Richard Henry Lee
- Thomas Jefferson
- Benjamin Harrison
- Thomas Nelson, Jr.
- Francis Lightfoot Lee
- Carter Braxton

Pennsylvania

- Robert Morris
- Benjamin Rush
- Benjamin Franklin
- John Morton
- George Clymer
- James Smith
- George Taylor
- James Wilson
- George Ross

Delaware

- Caesar Rodney
- George Read
- Thomas McKean

New York

- William Floyd
- Philip Livingston
- Francis Lewis

- Lewis Morris

New Jersey

- Richard Stockton
- John Witherspoon
- Francis Hopkinson
- John Hart
- Abraham Clark

New Hampshire

- Josiah Bartlett
- William Whipple
- Matthew Thornton
- Rhode Island
- Stephen Hopkins
- William Ellery

Connecticut

- Roger Sherman
- Samuel Huntington
- William Williams
- Oliver Wolcott

Other Hourglass Editions

"Hourglass Editions" condense world-changing books into approximately one hour of reading, without compromising the main storyline or message of the original work. We are always working to add new books to the lineup.

Check out other Hourglass Editions such as:

- "The Book of Mormon in One Hour"

Upcoming Hourglass Editions include:

- "The Gospels of the New Testament"
- "The Federalist Papers and US Constitution"

What new Hourglass Editions would you like to see? We hope to make an entire library of world-changing book abridgements, such as the ones below. Get involved, and share your opinions by reaching us at HourglassEditions@gmail.com

- "The Wealth of Nations" by Adam Smith
- "The Origin of Species" by Charles Darvin
- "Relativity" by Albert Einstein
- "Democracy in America" by Alexis de Tocqueville
- The Old Testament "Books of Moses" in One Hour
- "The Bible" abridged to a short story
- "The Doctrine and Covenants" in One Hour
- "The Talmud" in One Hour
- "The Hindu Vedas" in One Hour
- "The Qu'uran" in One Hour

Follow the progress of other Hourglass Edition projects using the links below:

On Facebook.com/HourglassEditions

On Instagram @HourglassEditions

Or point your phone's camera at the QR code below:

Made in the USA
Coppell, TX
12 February 2022